Creating
Terrific
TALKS

Creating Terrific TALKS

FOUR EASY STEPS

Virginia H. Pearce

DESERET
BOOK

SALT LAKE CITY, UTAH

The image on page 41, "Christ and the Children" by Harry Anderson © by Intellectual Reserve, Inc., is used with permission.

"I'm Trying to Be Like Jesus," reprinted on pages 22–23, is used with permission. © 1980 by Janice Kapp Perry.

Library of Congress Cataloging-in-Publication Data

Pearce, Virginia H.
   Creating terrific talks / Virginia H. Pearce.
      p.   cm.
   ISBN 1-57008-949-3 (Paperback)
   1. Public speaking—Study and teaching (Elementary)   I. Title.
   PN4086.P43   2003
   372.62'2—dc21   2003004432

Printed in the United States of America   72076-300241
Publishers Printing, Salt Lake City, Utah

10   9   8   7   6   5   4   3   2

✷ Table of Contents

✳ The Big Picture

I am fascinated by the story of Zion's Camp. Like a good mystery, the ending is completely unexpected and yet illuminates a truth that is a daily challenge in my life.

As you probably remember, Church membership in the winter of 1834 was spread between two main centers, one in Kirtland and one in Missouri. In Kirtland, the Saints were completely engaged in building the first temple of this dispensation. Joseph and Hyrum were on site and all was moving forward in a grand way.

In Missouri, however, mob persecution of the gathering Saints was increasing at a fearful rate. In February, Joseph Smith received a revelation directing him to gather a military force and march a thousand miles to secure Zion in Missouri. It was clear that this was the Lord's will (see D&C 103). The Saints were told to gather a force of five hundred; but if they couldn't get that many, one hundred would do. The Lord instructed Joseph Smith to go also to preside, organize, and "establish the children of Zion upon the laws and commandments which have been and which shall be given unto you" (D&C 103:35). He also promised, "All victory and glory is brought to pass unto you through your diligence, faithfulness, and prayers of faith" (D&C 103:36).

The task must have seemed very clear: With victory and glory in mind the two hundred men, eleven women, and seven children were to liberate the Saints from the tyranny of mobs. The prophet organized the camp in military fashion with groups of ten and fifty. They practiced military skills, obviously expecting to defeat the mobs and secure the future of the Church in Missouri at the end of their nine-hundred-mile march.

Well, they began to march. They got blisters, the food was poor, and the weather was bad. They began quarrelling among themselves, and many members of the camp blamed Joseph Smith for their discomfort. Some, suffering the same discomforts, still demonstrated great faith and kindliness. Somehow, for them, the journey itself became a great learning experience in which their faith and ability to persevere grew.

What happened to "The Task," the only reason some supposed they had suffered all of these discomforts? After weeks of marching, the night following their first encounter with a threatening mob, the Lord caused a great hailstorm. The mob dispersed. And then, at Fishing River, the Lord told Joseph that he was pleased the men had made the journey and accepted their sacrifice. But it was over. Zion's Camp had already served His purposes, which turned out to be quite different than the men of the camp had expected. His purpose, it seems, was to test and cultivate the faith and character of the individual men. The companies were disbanded and the members of the camp found their way back to Kirtland, sharing the gospel with those they met along the way. (See Joseph Smith, *History of The Church of Jesus Christ of Latter-day Saints*, 7 vols. 2nd ed. rev, ed. B. H. Roberts [Salt Lake City: The Church of Jesus Christ of Latter-day Saints, 1932–51], 2:61–134.)

Now, why do I like this story so much—a story that sort of fizzles and whimpers to an end? I'll tell you why: It is because this is the story of people who think that the task is the important thing and that however they behave on the way to doing it is inconsequential. And then the Lord clearly teaches them that sometimes tasks are meant only to be vehicles, means to give us an opportunity to develop personal qualities and attributes that are much more important than military victories.

And isn't that the eternal truth about the very purpose of our earthly experience? We recognize this grand truth in almost cliché fashion: It's not what you earn or accomplish in your career that counts. It's what you become by doing it. Elder Neal A. Maxwell talks often about those "portable" qualities that we must develop: patience, faith, integrity, and so on. They are portable because, unlike our daily tasks that seem to be the important thing, the qualities we develop as we set our hearts and minds to our work are the things that will be transported with us into the future and even beyond the grave.

If we were to carry this broadened view of our lives, would we do our tasks differently? I believe we would.

And that takes us to our work with children. As parents, we are literally blitzed by the tasks around us. Our children are required to accomplish many things each day. There is a math assignment with a deadline, a project due tomorrow, a discrete musical task to be practiced and conquered, a sport to master, a game to win, a bed to make, a Primary talk to be prepared and delivered. Those are just some of the tasks, and they are to be taken seriously. Like rescuing the beleaguered Saints in Missouri, these tasks are worthy of the time and energy of our children. However, what happens to the character and capacity of the individual child along the way is of far more lasting consequence than the completion of the task.

Perhaps one of the great joys of grandparenting is that we are removed from the multitude of task-oriented deadlines and we can actually see those portable qualities being developed. We can rejoice and reinforce the process, while parents are blinded by their immediate workload and seemingly more pressing deadlines.

This book is an effort to help teachers, parents, and children see Primary talks as more than an assignment to fill— just another deadline for adult and child. Rather, we can see a talk assignment as an opportunity to develop important, "portable" skills and attributes. We will rejoice in the process and use our time and energy in the most effective way to achieve the most important and lasting results.

Remember the Real Possibilities

There are many different ways for parents and teachers to help children prepare and present talks. Perhaps the most commonly used is for the adult to simply write a very short, simple talk—or get one from the *Friend* or another source— and help the child memorize it. This seems to be time efficient on the part of both parent and child. This method also increases predictability. For example, the parent knows exactly what the child is going to say—at least, what she is supposed to say—and should she falter, the parent knows exactly what to whisper. There is nothing wrong with this approach, but the question is this: Are there better ways? This becomes a pertinent question as we rethink the story of Zion's Camp and the real work that happened during the journey.

> " *Religious identity, or personal conversion, is one of the grand goals you will have an opportunity to move toward through helping a child prepare a Primary talk.* "

In other words, what positive things can happen along the way—for the child and for the audience? What qualities and skills can be developed that will have lasting value beyond this single assignment? What relationships can be strengthened? Can something as important as individual conversion become part of this process?

Research tells us that members, young and old, who become less active usually have not developed a personal identity with the gospel. Somehow it has always been outside of them—something that happens at church, in talks, or in lessons, but not something that informs their own thoughts, feelings, and behavior. Real conversion is the process of writing His law into the fleshy tablets of our hearts. Religious identity, or personal conversion, is one of the grand goals you will have an opportunity to move toward through helping a child prepare a Primary talk. This is big stuff—there really isn't anything much bigger.

As you contemplate this grand process, an important question to be asking yourself is: *Do I believe that my child has the capacity to understand and articulate her understanding of gospel principles?* If you believe she does not, you are probably wrong. A child's understanding of truth is usually much greater than her ability to give words to that understanding. And so an important part of the Big Picture is to recognize the role that you, the adult, can play most effectively. You are not the thinker of the ideas, the writer of the talk, the responsible party; rather, the child and her thoughts and feelings are the center of the picture and you are merely her assistant. The key is for a parent to see himself or herself as someone who can gently ask questions that will help the child put words to what she already knows and feels.

This little book will guide the reader through the journey of helping a child prepare and present a talk. The process will be broken down into four main steps: (1) exploring, (2) creating, (3) practicing, and (4) presenting.

✳ ✳ ✳
Religious Identity

This is who I am inside, to the core: A believing member of The Church of Jesus Christ of Latter-day Saints. I am a member who has had experiences with God that have resulted in a spiritual witness of the truthfulness of the gospel. I am a member who recognizes the benefits of living the gospel and has confidence in the goodness of God. I am a member who feels accepted in the congregation of Saints, who has the skills and the confidence to contribute to the lives of the members of my ward. God and His work are the center of my world.

✳ Step One

EXPLORING

Eight-year-old Sam came home with a slip of paper inviting him to give a talk next Sunday. His wise mother didn't see it simply as an assignment; she saw it as a personal invitation to talk about, read about, and think about the gospel with her son. Slowing him down with a hug and a scoop onto her lap, she said, "This is great. We'll have a good time thinking about this one. Hmmm. It says that the theme this month is tithing. Let's talk about tithing tonight when I tuck you in to bed. This is going to be a good one!" Sam responded to her high five and hit the floor running.

That night, as she tucked Sam into bed and turned to go, he said, "Wait. I thought we were going to do my talk!"

"Oh, I forgot," Mom said as she sat down on the edge of his bed.

They began to talk. At least, Mother found ways for Sam to talk. She began by saying, "Tell me everything you know about tithing."

She listened carefully, helping him to keep talking past the obvious. She prompted him with, "What else?" "Can you tell me more about that?" "Finish this sentence: 'Tithing is like . . . ' or 'Tithing reminds me of . . . ' " "When you paid your tithing for the first time, how did you do it, how did you feel?" "Tell me about it."

When they finished talking, Mother said, "You know a lot about tithing, Sam. Let's just kneel down again before you go to bed and ask Heavenly Father to help us as we keep working on it so that you will be able to talk about tithing in the way He wants you to." The prayer was a short but sweet end to one of those little ten-minute conversations that are what happy family life is all about.

> **"***The initial conversation about the talk subject should be in a relaxed setting.***"**

The Exploring Conversation

The initial conversation about the talk subject should be in a relaxed setting. Sam and his mother were enjoying that winding-down time before sleep. But there are multiple other settings that could support a casual and relaxed conversation. You may find that riding in the car with the child, going for a walk, doing routine chores like the dishes or preparing dinner are all good places to do this initial exploring.

As you begin the exploring phase, remember that one of the great possibilities of this whole process is an opportunity to further develop a positive relationship with your child. This won't be automatic, however. Remember the folks of Zion's Camp who reacted to the stresses of the journey by becoming irritated and critical of one another? Don't let that happen to you. Don't allow the talk to become just another stressor. What would be the long-term consequences if every time a Church assignment were received it was only after pressure, prodding, and unpleasantness?

Consciously make a choice to slow down and attend to the child. One-on-one, unhurried time with a parent is a simple but life-sustaining gift. Take advantage of a talk assignment to give that gift to your child.

The exploring time can also be a time when you help the child know that this little project is one in which you want to include the Lord at every step, so that He can actually help you, through the Holy Ghost, to understand things in a way you couldn't understand otherwise.

Exploring, by definition, takes time. Exploring is not finding the most direct route between two points; it is wandering around just a little in new territory. When we explore we become discoverers. Most of us are not very good at helping children by giving them time and space to find the words and name the feelings. Casually but firmly slowing down and holding onto this beginning part of the process will reassure your child that thinking about and talking about the gospel are important things he is grown-up enough to do.

The longer you stay with the exploring part of the process, the better the final talk will be and the better chance for the development of portable skills, qualities, and attributes.

Beginning with the Child

No matter where the exploring conversation takes place, remember to go where the child is and follow him where he goes. Let him be in charge of the conversation. Your child's heart and mind are the entry points for talk preparation. Parents who see themselves as the all-knowing chalk and the child as the empty slate are missing out on developing a warm relationship based on mutual respect.

If you begin by taking your child to your thoughts/experiences/favorite scriptures, or to someone else's, you will miss the opportunity to develop your child's religious identity and assist in his real conversion.

So begin with the child. Encourage him to add on, to tell you more. Help him know that he is the most important player in this game. Ask questions: "Tell me again." "Have you ever had an experience with . . . ?" "Where were you when that happened?" "How were you feeling?" "What else was happening?" "What happened next?" "How?" "Why do you think you felt that way?"

Thinking, real thinking—not just popping off "the right answer" from the top of your head and moving to the next question—can be developed right from the beginning of the preparation time. Asking follow-up questions will help the child to think more deeply. Asking questions like, "Does that remind you of anything else?" or using Sam's mother's prompt, "Tithing is like . . ." will help your child link ideas together, another important thinking skill.

As your conversation goes on, you may feel that your child seems to be talking about something that might seem quite boring or irrelevant to you. Keep this judgment to yourself and try to find out why the idea is important to him. Listen as intently as you can.

Sometimes we think we already know what children are feeling and thinking and what they need to say and do. Therefore, we think it would be helpful if we just got more efficient with this whole thing and imparted some of our vast store of wisdom and knowledge, got a little backup from "the books," and checked this task off our list.

There will be some silences, some "I dunnos." Resist the impulse to fill those silences with your own answers. Try to sense when he just needs more thinking time or when he needs you to rephrase or change the question.

If you let the child take the lead, you are likely—after one or two encounters—to feel that sweet Spirit that comes when two souls discuss a gospel truth as deeply and personally as they are able to find the words to do so. But your child will have to be well into the dialogue before you begin to take part in any way except by asking questions and supporting the hesitant beginnings. Taking the time and effort necessary to protect thinking and talking space for ourselves and our children will bring a harvest—a harvest of children who know and do what is right.

Beginning with What Is Happening Right Now in the Child's Life

One of the simplest ways to begin with the child, and probably one of the most effective, is to begin with what is happening—actual events—in his life right now, then move immediately into what is going on inside the child in reaction to these events.

When nine-year-old Sarah came home with a talk assignment, her mother began with Sarah's life. "Sarah," she said, "We're moving to California in a few weeks. What have you been thinking about when we talk about moving? Is there anything you have been especially worried about?"

"Of course," replied Sarah.

"Well . . . ?"

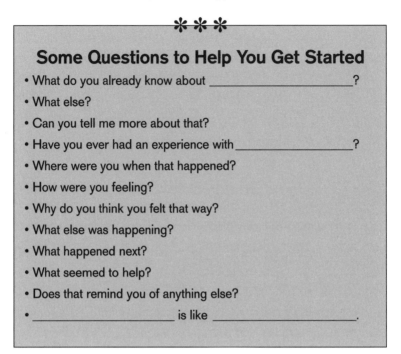

* * *

Some Questions to Help You Get Started

- What do you already know about _____?
- What else?
- Can you tell me more about that?
- Have you ever had an experience with _____?
- Where were you when that happened?
- How were you feeling?
- Why do you think you felt that way?
- What else was happening?
- What happened next?
- What seemed to help?
- Does that remind you of anything else?
- _____ is like _____.

"Well, I'm worried about if the kids at the new school will be nice, and my new teacher, and stuff like that."

Mother hugged her and said, "Of course those would be things you are worried about. Let me give you a piece of paper. Start out by writing, 'We are moving.' Then write down some of the things you are worried about."

Sarah wrote:

> We are moving.
>
> And there are a lot of questions I have, like Is my teacher going to be nice? Will there be any bullies? Will I make new friends? Will my principal be nice? Will my street be nice?
>
> Those are all my questions. All of these questions make me feel worried.

We are moving. And there are a lot of questions I have like.....
Is my teacher going to be nice, will there be any bullies, will I make new friends, will my principal be nice, will my street be nice? Those are all my questions. All of these questions make me feel worried.

Sarah's mom helped her come up with a talk topic by discussing a current event in Sarah's life.

Sarah's mother knew, of course, that moving is a little scary for all of us; but when she saw Sarah's fears written out on paper, her heart swelled with love and respect for this brave little girl. "Sarah," she said softly, "What will help you with all of these worries?"

Sarah looked up, "Well, maybe I could take a picture of you to school with me and put it in my desk so I could look at it when I feel scared. And I could get extra hugs from you and Dad when I get home from school every day."

"Oh, those are great ideas. Dad and I can love you and help you. We are all going to need to help each other—we are a little bit scared too. Who else loves us and can help us?"

Sarah thought for a moment, and then said, "Heavenly Father! He can help people no matter where they are."

"Isn't it wonderful! That's why Dad and I pray every morning and every night and lots of times in between."

Sarah's face lit up. "Hey, that's a talk!" she exclaimed. "I could give my talk about praying and how Heavenly Father makes you know that everything will be okay," and she quickly began to write about prayer underneath her list of worries.

Beginning with Other Resources

Beginning with the child doesn't mean that you can't begin with other resources. But as you introduce the resource, you will still want to begin with the child's reaction to it.

Beginning with a Picture

A Primary teacher found herself a week ahead on the lessons. With the extra time she decided to give her class of ten-year-olds an opportunity to individually prepare a talk. She didn't tell the class what she was doing because she didn't want them to run straight to the task: quickly find a subject, superficially scribble down something, and "finish first." And so she kept Missouri secret from her Zion's Camp trekkers.

She found several photographs from magazines and other sources and hung them around the room. She asked the children to quietly look at each picture until they each found one that was particularly interesting. Since this would have to be very individual and require some quiet thinking and feeling time, the teacher asked the children not to talk.

When they had all made a choice she wrote this beginning on the chalkboard:

I chose the picture of _____ because _____ .

She then asked them to go to work on their papers. While they were working she noticed those who were having trouble and began asking them gentle questions: "What do you like about the picture?" "What do you think is happening?" "How are the people feeling?" "Can you write some of those things on your paper?"

Coaxing the children's thinking along, she asked them to look at the picture again and make a connection to themselves. Then she wrote on the chalkboard:

Sometimes I am _____ or

Once I _____ .

This was getting easier now, and most of the children could think of things to talk about and write about. More children wanted to talk, and the teacher tried to allow them to do that because she knew their minds were beginning to engage and they needed something faster than a pencil to keep up with the sorting and sifting process.

Now came the jump. On the board the teacher wrote:

Heavenly Father _____ or

In the scriptures _____ .

What? They all were puzzled. "What do you mean?"

Finally she said, "Let's make your ideas into a talk now."

"Oh," they said. "We get it! We need a scripture story or something."

Together the class slowly began to name some of the scripture stories they had learned that year: Esther, Daniel, Jonah, and so on. As they went through them, suddenly a little body would jump into action. "That's a story that will work for me! Do you want me to write it down?"

"Yes. Just what you can remember and what will help us to think about what you have already written."

"But I can't think of a story that fits," said one of the girls.

"Well, then, what about the Topical Guide? Could we look up a word together that might help?" asked the teacher.

And the girl was off and running.

This is what Stewart wrote:

> I chose the picture of the little kid because when I looked at it the picture just stood out and he just looked confused, worried, and sad.
>
> Sometimes I am confused, worried, and sad, like when my dog had been lost for almost a whole day and then we found her in Sandy. When we are sad, worried, and confused we can always pray for guidance.
>
> ~~Like in Daniel and the lions' den. Daniel was wor-~~ shipping Heavenly Father, and the king said, "Stop or you'll be thrown in the lions' den." Even though he said that, Daniel kept on praying and worshipping, so then the king threw him in the den. Daniel probably felt sad,

Stewart's teacher encouraged him to use his reaction to the above picture to build the talk below.

I chose this picture of the little kid because when I looked at it the picture just stood out. He looked confused, worried, and sad. Like when my dog had been lost for almost a whole day and then we found her in Sandy. When we are sad, worried, or confused we can always pray for guidance. Like in Daniel and the Lion's Den. Daniel was worshipping Heavenly Father, but the king said stop, or you'll be thrown in the lion's den. Even though he said that, Daniel kept on praying and worshipping. So then the king threw him in the den. Daniel probably felt sad, worried, and confused but Heavenly Father shut the lion's mouths so they couldn't harm him. When you're lacking guidance you can always pray.

worried, and confused, but Heavenly Father shut the lions' mouths so they wouldn't hurt him.

When you're lacking guidance you can always pray.

Beginning with a Scripture Verse

Another place to begin with a child would be with a scripture verse; but remember, it's still about the child—what scripture he responds to, not one of your favorites!

Catherine came into the chapel from Primary wildly waving a slip of paper in her father's face.

"Whoa, what's going on here?" he said as he ducked and dodged his constantly in motion six-year-old.

"It's a talk, Dad. They picked me. I get to give one next week!"

"Well, let's see what this very important piece of paper says then," he whispered, as he pulled her onto the bench beside him, waiting for sacrament meeting to begin.

"Hmm," he said. "Looks like they have four steps here: '(1) choose a scripture, (2) explain what it means, (3) share a personal experience or story, and (4) bear your testimony.' We'll talk about it after church, but maybe during sacrament meeting you'd like to look at my scriptures. Just quietly go through them, especially the parts that are underlined. You won't be able to read them all, but I'll help you when we get home to find one you like. Yeah, the choosing part will be a fun place to start. And let's be sure to pray about your choice, so you will feel that it is the one that would please Heavenly Father, too."

Even though these Primary leaders gave Catherine an outline, detailing that the child should begin with a scripture,

Catherine's wise father let her make the first move. At a more opportune moment (after sacrament meeting), he was willing to allow time to help her explore and find a scripture that would be her choice, not someone else's.

Beginning with a Scripture Story

Beginning with a scripture verse is quite different than beginning with a scripture story. When they began working on seven-year-old Mandy's talk, her mother asked her to write down her favorite scripture story. She thought for just a moment before she said, "I know. The iron rod. And I want to write the whole talk right now!" This is what she wrote:

> **Lehi had a dream about a lot of people holding on to the iron rod. Some did not because people in the big building made fun of them. Jesus said, "Hold on to what you believe in." I believe in listening to the talk**

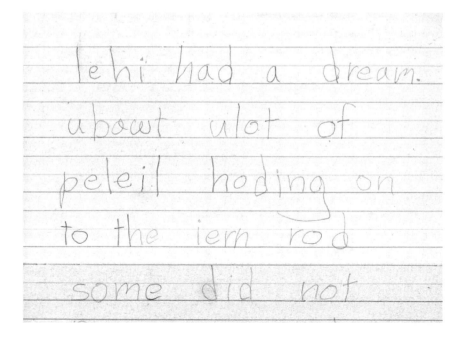

Because peipl in the Big billding made fun uf them geises sied hod on to wut you Bleivin

I Bleivin in lisning

to the tock in

Sackritmeiting

wat I wood Bleivin

the 10 cmanßihs

in the Name in ceises

amen

Mandy's mom encouraged her to tell her favorite scripture story in a talk.

in sacrament meeting. I believe in the ten commandments. In the name of Jesus Christ, Amen.

Beginning with a Theme or Topic

Now, what about the Primary assignment that comes
home with a designated theme or specific scripture? You can
still begin with the child.

Four-year-old Rebecca's invitation to give a talk the next
Sunday indicated that the theme in Primary for the month
was "I'll Follow Him in Faith" (Galatians 3:26, "For ye are all
the children of God by faith in Christ Jesus").

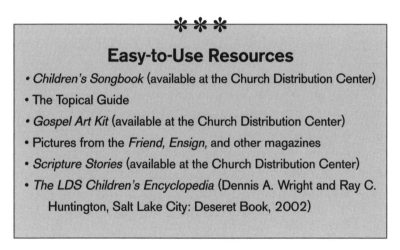

✳ ✳ ✳
Easy-to-Use Resources

- *Children's Songbook* (available at the Church Distribution Center)
- The Topical Guide
- *Gospel Art Kit* (available at the Church Distribution Center)
- Pictures from the *Friend, Ensign,* and other magazines
- *Scripture Stories* (available at the Church Distribution Center)
- *The LDS Children's Encyclopedia* (Dennis A. Wright and Ray C.
  Huntington, Salt Lake City: Deseret Book, 2002)

"Hmmm," Rebecca's mother said thoughtfully. "This is a
good one, Rebecca, because you already know a lot about
following Jesus. I think you even know a song. See if you can
guess!"

Mom began to hum "I'm Trying to Be Like Jesus."
Rebecca's face lit up.

"Sing it with me," Mom coaxed, and Rebecca joined
right in.

I'm Trying to Be like Jesus

By this time Mother was sitting comfortably on a chair. She lifted Rebecca into a position facing her directly, her legs straddling her mother's lap. "Now, sweetheart, let's play a game. I'm going to sing the song again and you listen carefully for the words you like the most. When we come to words you like, hold up both your hands and I'll stop singing."

The first time through the song, it was ridiculous! Rebecca held up her hands every few words. Undaunted,

he did, in all that I do and say. At I
glad - ness when Je - sus will come a - gain.

times I am tempt-ed to make a wrong choice, But I try to lis - ten as the
try to re-mem-ber the les-sons he taught. Then the Ho - ly Spir - it en-ters

still small voice whis-pers, "Love one an-oth - er as Je - sus loves you.
in - to my thoughts, say-ing:

Try to show kind-ness in all that you do. Be gen - tle and lov - ing in

deed and in thought, For these are the things Je-sus taught." 2. I'm taught."

Words and music: Janice Kapp Perry, b. 1938
Copyright © 1980 by Janice Kapp Perry. This song may be copied for incidental,
noncommercial church or home use.

John 13:15, 34

Mother laughed, but each time Rebecca held up her hands Mother stopped and they talked a little about the phrase of words and what it meant.

"Okay, let's do it again. And this time you can choose only one time and it might be at the very end of the song, in the middle of the song, or at the beginning. In fact, I won't sing the song, I'll just say it so that you can think more about the words. Ready?"

Rebecca's eyes twinkled and she had her hands ready, but she waited and waited until Mother got to the words, "Try to show kindness in all that you do." Then up the hands went as she giggled in delight.

"Oh, what a good choice! That is a great way to follow Jesus. Let's tell the other Primary children about that."

During the getting-started time an alert parent will be listening carefully in order to get a sense of what is interesting and compelling to the child, what seems to have enough meaning to him that it will be worth telling someone else about. One way you will know that you have spent enough time in the exploring phase is when you can answer yes to the following questions: Is he interested in what he is talking about? Does it seem important to him? Is he, rather than you, carrying the energy of the conversation?

✼ Step Two

CREATING THE TALK

Once you've taken some time to explore, the job is to help your child actually create a talk. Like Mandy and Stewart, some children will have immediately taken a paper and pencil and written out a talk during the exploration phase. In the creating phase, you will want to ask your child to read out loud what she has written, asking her if there are any parts she would like to add, take away, or change. Some children will immediately begin to fill in and refine, but most could use some simple directions during the creating phase.

One Idea

There are a number of simple models you can use as you help your child create her talk. You have probably invented some yourself without realizing it. I will illustrate a few in this chapter; but central to each model is One Idea—the identification of one gospel concept. Sometimes the One Idea may have been decided as part of the invitation to speak. But even when it has been identified, your child, through exploring, will have personalized that idea. If the idea has been designated, this is the time to mesh the given topic with whatever compels your child. Remember back to the exploring conversations. Ask yourself, *Where did my child's interest seem to have the most energy?*

Do the same thing with a scripture. (Although it may seem like the One Idea is already there, it isn't. Every scripture contains *many* ideas, many directions for thought.) Have your child respond to open-ended questions, such as, "What do you think Heavenly Father meant when he said that?" or "What is Alma trying to teach us here?" Her answers will lead you to helping her identify the One Idea, or topic sentence.

Exploring a song will yield the same results. Four-year-old Rebecca identified her excitement about the phrase, "Try to show kindness in all that you do." The topic given, however, was "I'll Follow Him in Faith," so Mother began to talk about faith, but she soon could see she had lost Rebecca's attention. Immediately regrouping, Mother dropped the words of the theme and went back to Rebecca's choice: "Try to show kindness in all that you do."

"Tell me some ways that you have been kind today," she said. Then, "How did you feel when you were kind?" The central Big Idea for Rebecca was simply that Jesus wants us to be kind. At her maturity level (remember, she is four years old), talking about faith, it's definition, and implications would probably be unproductive. The specific words in an assigned topic are important only so far as the child's maturity allows her to understand them. To sacrifice talking about what she does know and feel so that she can talk in the specified language of the topic is counterproductive for both the child and her audience, who will sense her lack of understanding and interest in a concept and feel the same lack of interest.

Wise Primary leaders will be aware of a child's level of understanding when they assign speaking parts in the annual children's sacrament meeting presentation. Care and time should be taken to have every child speak her part—no matter how long or short—in her own vocabulary and congruent with her own experience and understanding.

> **"***Care and time should be taken to have every child speak her part— no matter how long or short—in her own vocabulary and congruent with her own experience and understanding.***"**

The One Idea should be quite specific because a Primary talk is brief; the speaker won't be giving an exhaustive discussion of a gospel principle, just talking about the facet of that principle that has the most personal meaning to her right now.

The child could use the One Idea as the beginning sentence of the talk and perhaps throughout. She will surely use it in the conclusion of the talk.

Thinking about the Audience

During the exploring stage, parents are immersed in the child—her thoughts, her life experience, and her feelings. Conversations during that time help the child put words to those things. After the slow exploring time, however, it's time to think about the talk itself. With that comes an awareness of those to whom your child will be speaking. What are the audience's concerns, life experiences, and capacity to understand? What is it your child feels strongly about (the One

Idea) that might have meaning for individuals in the audience? It's unwise to belabor this with a child, but parents can easily give a gentle reminder now and again, such as, "Rebecca, I'll bet even the older children in Primary sometimes have trouble being kind. Your talk

> **"** *The ability to put yourself into the head and heart of someone else is a slowly acquired but critical attribute of a spiritually mature adult.* **"**

will be helpful to them." That's all that need be said to Rebecca, a four-year-old; but it nudges her toward a mature understanding of the needs and interests of others. Remember that you are trying to build in some long-term, portable attributes and skills during this giving-a-Primary-talk process. The ability to put yourself into the head and heart of someone else is a slowly acquired but critical attribute of a spiritually mature adult.

Using Supporting Material to Illustrate the One Idea

The best material to illustrate an idea, especially when we are talking about building internal connections to gospel principles, is always our own—our own experiences, our own feelings, our own confirmations of gospel truths. Our own experience is not only powerful to us but is also a key to the hearts of the audience members. Remember the audience we just mentioned? What will help audience members understand and receive a witness of this One Idea? Hearing an honest personal experience always invites us as listeners to think of our own experiences. As a speaker talks about what he knows because of his experience, he is in effect bearing his testimony of the principle, thereby inviting the Holy Ghost to witness. Herein lies the power of speaking and teaching one another. If we fail to invite the Spirit, in essence, we cannot teach one another. "If ye receive not the Spirit ye shall not teach" (D&C 42:14).

Stewart's personal experience of being confused, worried, and sad when his dog was lost; Sarah's worries about a new school; Rebecca's sudden excitement as she identified a phrase in the song—these are the essential elements of the talks. Without giving expression to these personal feelings, we are marching with Zion's Camp yet choosing to ignore the real potential for individual conversion and growth. We are also decreasing the likelihood that the other children and adults in the audience will feel the witness of the Spirit and increase their testimonies.

Benjamin was eleven years old and fiercely independent. He casually informed his family on Saturday night that he was supposed to give a talk in Primary tomorrow. Mother tried very hard not to let the panic show on her face because experience had taught her that if her anxiety level went up, Benjamin retreated immediately. So, just as casually, keeping her eyes on the dinner dishes she was doing, she asked Benjamin what he had decided to speak about.

"Ah, I dunno." Silence. "They said it has to be about the sacrament."

Once again Mother held back, let a few moments pass, and then said, "Sounds like a good topic since you'll be passing the sacrament yourself in a few months."

No response. Mother kept doing the dishes and Benjamin ambled out of the room.

In about twenty minutes, Mother pulled *The LDS Children's Encyclopedia* (Dennis Wright and Ray Huntington, Salt Lake City: Deseret Book, 2002) from the bookshelf, marked the sacrament entry with a bookmark, and took the scriptures from the end table, marking the sacrament entry in the Topical Guide.

Benjamin was throwing a ball against the side of the house. She went outside and stood in between him and the house, caught the next throw, and tossed the ball back. The next time she caught it, she turned toward the house and said, "I found some things you might want to use." Benjamin followed her into the house.

"Oh, I'm almost finished," he bluffed.

"Great!" she said, as she handed him the books. "Still it might be a good time to read the sacrament entry in the *Encyclopedia* to see if there is anything you want to add to your talk or look in the Topical Guide for a scripture to end with. More important than the books, though, is what you think about the sacrament—just one idea about the sacrament that you think is important.

"And Benjamin," she called over her shoulder as she left the room, "you might want to practice your talk on Anne. I'm going to put her in the bathtub in about an hour and it would help me if you could stay in the bathroom to tend her while she plays in the water. And she'd be a great audience!"

Benjamin disappeared. The next day his mother slipped into the back of the Primary room with a trembling heart. She was amazed and touched to hear Benjamin carefully explain the importance of the sacrament, using the language of the sacrament prayer and closing with a simple testimony.

Models for Illustrating the One Idea

Most children will welcome more guidance than Benjamin. After the One Idea is identified there is an endless number of models that can simplify the creation or structuring of the talk. Here are five easy possibilities:

- The Stepping-Stairs Model
- The Webbing of Circles Model
- The Prompts Model
- The Four-Square Model
- The Conversation Model

The Stepping-Stairs Model

In the stepping-stairs model, every vertical stair is a statement or restatement of the main idea. In between each

* * *

Resources to Illustrate the One Idea

- Scriptures, including the Topical Guide and Bible Dictionary
- The *Friend*
- *The Church News*
- The *Ensign* or *New Era*
- Family history stories
- Personal stories
- *The LDS Children's Encyclopedia* (Dennis Wright and Ray Huntington, Salt Lake City: Deseret Book, 2002)
- Poems
- Stories from literature (from books such as *The Book of Virtues* [William J. Bennett, New York: Simon and Schuster, 1993])
- *Gospel Art Kit* (available at the Church Distribution Center)

vertical line is a horizontal stair, where the main idea is illustrated more fully.

The stairs model can help the child keep firmly on track with the One Idea, since every vertical step is a restatement of the idea. The horizontal messages can be anything from a scripture, personal example, or definition from the dictionary to a statement from a published resource, such as *The LDS Children's Encyclopedia* (Wright and Huntington, 2002), a quote from one of the General Authorities, or any number of other sources.

Remember Sarah, who was about to move? Sarah identified the main idea herself when she said, "Hey, that's a talk! I could give my talk about praying and how Heavenly Father makes you know that everything will be okay." To help her organize and expand the talk, Mother could draw some large stairs across a paper. Then she could easily say, turning the paper, "Yes, write that down on this first vertical step: "When we pray, Heavenly Father can help us know that everything will be okay."

On the first horizontal step, Sarah wrote, "Moving to California—my worries."

Turning the paper to write on the next vertical step, she asked Sarah to write again: "When I pray, Heavenly Father helps me know that everything will be okay."

On the next horizontal step, Sarah wrote, "My mother and dad pray about their worries, like. . . ."

On the next vertical step she asked Sarah to write, "When my mother and dad pray, Heavenly Father helps them know that everything will be okay."

On the next horizontal line, Sarah wrote, "The scriptures say or our Prophet says . . ." and then they decided to look

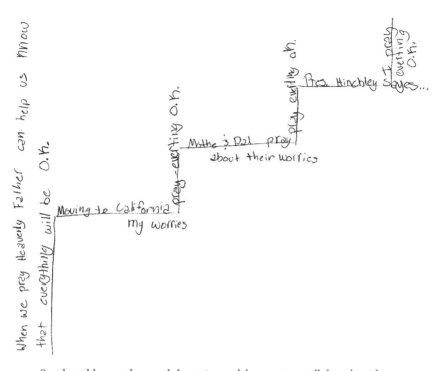

*Sarah and her mother used the stairs model to create a talk based on the
idea that Heavenly Father helps us to know everything will be okay.
Each step on the model reinforced Sarah's One Idea.*

in *Teachings of Gordon B. Hinckley* (Salt Lake City: Deseret
Book, 1997) under the entry on prayer. They read two or
three paragraphs together. Sarah chose to write on the next
horizontal step: "President Hinckley said: 'Be prayerful. . . .
You need the help of your Father in Heaven who loves you
and wants you to succeed and be happy'" (*Teachings of
Gordon B. Hinckley*, 469).

On the last vertical step, Sarah restated the One Idea in
the form of her testimony, "I have prayed lots of times when
I am worried, and Heavenly Father always helps everything
to turn out okay."

The stairs model can include just one or two stairs or lots

of stairs, depending on the amount of time available, the age of the child, and the attention span of the audience. A very young child may want only two or three steps with very briefly stated examples on the horizontal steps. An older child may choose to use five or six steps or just spend more time with each of two or three steps by telling a scripture story or a personal story in more detail or spending a few sentences talking about a particular quote from a Church leader.

The final vertical step should always be a restatement of the One Idea in the form of a personal testimony, summarizing the idea as well as inviting the Holy Ghost to testify of its truthfulness.

The stepping-stairs model is helpful when the child practices and presents her talk because it doesn't allow enough space to write every word, but serves as a reminder of sequence and ideas.

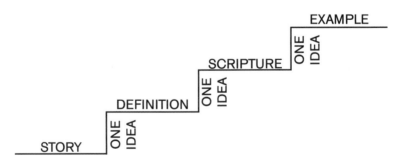

However many steps, or however long each segment is, the stepping-stairs model is a disciplined way for children or adults to keep themselves and their audience focused on one important idea as they illustrate it through personal stories, scriptures, words of the prophets, and testimony.

The Webbing of Circles Model

Another model involves the webbing of circles of ideas and/or resources. In this model we write the One Idea in a circle in the center of the paper, then draw spokes out to other circles where we place related ideas and possibilities.

Remember eight-year-old Sam and his mother having a bedtime chat about tithing, a topic assigned by the Primary presidency? A couple of days later Sam was finishing a snack at the kitchen table. Seizing the moment with a rarely still child, Mother grabbed a paper and pencil and sat down beside him. "Let's think some more about your talk, Sam. How about drawing it like this?" she said as she drew a circle in the middle of the page.

Now, Sam's mother had noticed that in their exploring Sam seemed to show the most interest when they began talking about his own experience paying tithing, and especially the process of what happens to tithing. Inside the circle she had him write, "Paying my tithing."

"Does that seem like a good title for your talk?"

"Sure," said Sam, and stuffed another cookie in his mouth. Sam's mother seemed to have hit on the One Idea. By visually putting it in the center of the circle, she helped Sam to see that everything he talks about should help with the One Idea.

Next Sam's mother started to draw spokes out from the circle and connect them to other circles.

"Now, what were some of the things you said about paying tithing when we were talking the other night?" They began to review together their earlier conversation, putting

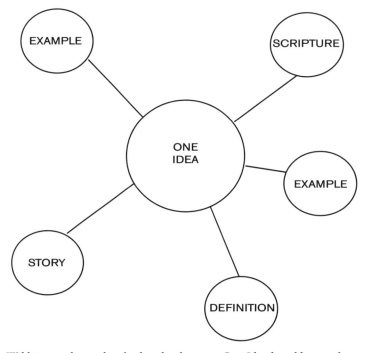

Webbing can be used to further develop your One Idea by adding circles that contain examples, stories, scriptures, and so on. The beginnings of Sam's talk are in the model below

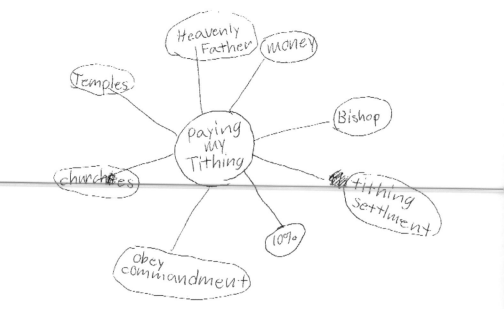

spokes out from the circle with some of the ideas they could remember.

After they put down all the ideas they could remember, she let Sam choose which ones to cross out, leaving the two or three that he wanted to talk about.

Sam's mom wrapped things up with, "I think this will be a good talk to give because it could help the children who haven't paid tithing yet to know how to do it and why." Did you notice how Sam's mother helped him gently anticipate the needs of the audience?

The Prompts Model

Sentence stubs are unfinished sentences that serve as useful prompts in the exploring phase, but they can also form a structure for creating the talk.

Stewart's Primary teacher helped her class members actually create their talks during the exploring phase by completing a series of three sequential sentence stubs.

1. I chose the picture of _____ because _____.

2. Sometimes I am _____.

3. Heavenly Father _____ or in the scriptures _____.

Notice that as Stewart completed the sentence stubs he automatically verbalized his One Idea—When we are confused, worried, or sad we can pray—three times: in the beginning, in the middle, and at the end. That repetition will allow the audience members to clearly hear and remember the message.

I chose this picture of the little kid because when I looked at it the picture just stood out. He looked confused, worried, and sad. Like when my dog had been lost for almost a whole day and then we found her in Sandy. When we are sad, worried, or confused we can always pray for guidance. Like in Daniel and the Lion's Den. Daniel was worshipping Heavenly Father, but the king said stop, or you'll be thrown in the lion's den. Even though he said that, Daniel kept on praying and worshipping. So then the king threw him in the den. Daniel probably felt sad, worried, and confused but Heavenly Father shut the lion's mouths so they couldn't harm him. When you're lacking guidance you can always pray.

The message in Stewart's talk—his One Idea—is verbalized three times, helping his audience clearly understand what Stewart wants to say.

The Four-Square Model

The four-square method is a simple way for a child of any age to organize her talk. It has four discrete steps: (1) choose a favorite scripture, (2) explain what you think Heavenly Father is trying to teach with the scripture, (3) give an example of this in your life, and (4) bear your testimony about the principle.

Catherine's Primary presidency sent her home with this four-square model:

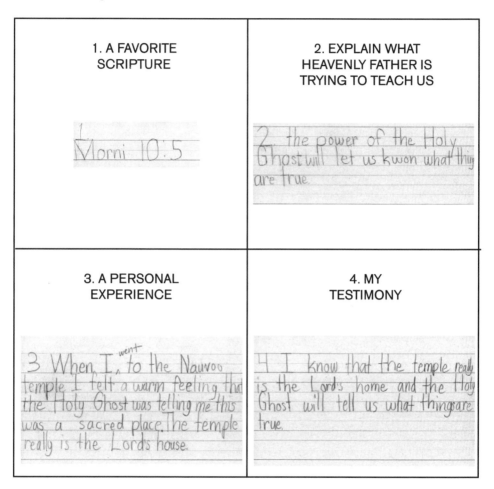

This may feel like a sterile formula, but when you begin with the child it can be powerful. Let her choose the scripture, help her explore its meaning, help her connect her own life experience to the scripture, and then close with a personal testimony. This is a powerful and simple model. No wonder a Primary leader offered it!

The Conversation Model

Now, what about creating a talk when the child is shy and very young and you anticipate that she will have difficulty even standing at the pulpit alone? After all, in this remarkable church three-, four-, and five-year-olds are asked to teach us! That is a wondrous practice, based on the doctrinal realities of the worth and capacity of children. "And now, he imparteth his word by angels unto men, yea, not only men but women also. Now this is not all; little children do have words given unto them many times, which confound the wise and the learned" (Alma 32:23).

One very simple model to use with young children is the conversation. Jonathan was four years old, and this would be his first talk. Mother went through the *Gospel Art Kit* and found a picture of Christ and the children. They looked at the picture carefully together, Mother asking questions about every single detail. In this exploring phase, she listened carefully to Jonathan, noticing that he was particularly interested in the way Jesus was listening to the little boy, putting his arm around him, and looking at him. As they talked, she felt Jonathan grow reverent when he said that it looked like Jesus loved the boy. Mother felt that this would be the One Idea—Jesus loves children. So when they began to create the talk, she re-created that part of their conversation. When it was time to present the talk, she went to the pulpit with him, held up the picture, and the talk was given as a conversation between the two of them, with the audience listening in:

"Jonathan, who is in this picture?"

"That is Jesus and those are children."

"What is Jesus doing?"

"Talking to the children."

"How do you think Jesus feels about those children?"

"He cares about them 'cause he is listening to them."

"How does he feel about you?"

"He loves me."

"How do you feel about him?"

"I love him."

"In the name of Jesus Christ, amen."

Jonathan had a successful experience expressing his thoughts in the comfort of a model that allowed his mother to be beside him while he delivered his own message.

✳ Step Three
PRACTICING THE TALK

Communicating vs. Memorizing

In Stewart's Primary class, where the teacher helped the children build talks from their reactions to pictures, there was time for each child to present his talk. One by one the ten-year-old children stood and read from their papers. The children stumbled over their own handwriting, they mumbled and kept their eyes glued to the paper, the class-member audience was restless. When they had all finished, the teacher said, "Those were very good messages. Now let's talk about giving them. What do you think?"

Several children began to talk at the same time. They all agreed that reading talks just doesn't work. Surprisingly enough, they all quickly volunteered that memorizing talks wasn't a good idea either.

"Why?" the teacher asked.

"Well, because if you forget one word you get all mixed up and the whole thing is ruined!" volunteered one boy. They all nodded their heads in agreement.

"Then what do you do?" the teacher asked this class of experts.

Natalie said that she writes her talk down, then reads it out loud to her mother over and over and over, "about 20 times." After that she takes five or six cards and writes just one or two key words on each card, never a whole sentence. "Then it's easy," she said. "You don't forget the order of the ideas, and you can just tell the talk to the other kids."

So "telling the talk" becomes the goal. Now you are really helping the child to think about the audience. Stewart will want to tell the other children about his lost dog. They will understand just how he felt because most of them have lost something very precious at some time. The teacher or parent who wants to coach him can say, "Be sure to look at someone, someone who will want to know about your dog, and think about explaining to him how you felt."

Telling the talk over and over again in the mirror is a good idea. Also, invite the child to tell the talk to brothers and sisters, even the baby. You will remember that Benjamin's mother knew from past experience that he wanted to prepare and practice his talk alone—without parental help—so she gently suggested he practice on his little sister.

The younger child will usually be happy to have parents involved in the practicing. When he is practicing the telling and leaves parts out, don't give him the words to say; instead, ask questions to prompt his memory, such as, "How did you feel when you lost the dog?" This works much better than saying, "You forgot to say, 'When we are sad, worried, and confused we can always pray for guidance.'"

Nine-year-old Elizabeth wanted to tell the scripture story of David and Goliath as the main part of her talk on courage.

During the exploring part of the process, Elizabeth's mother got out the scriptures and together they read the seventeenth chapter of First Samuel. They read it slowly, in a relaxed way. In fact, it took them two or three sessions to read the whole chapter because they would talk about the words Elizabeth didn't understand, measure out on a wall how tall Goliath would have been, and so on. They even drew pictures of what happened as they went along. It was a way of taking notes. You see, Elizabeth's mother recognized an opportunity to burn this wondrous story right into the heart of her daughter—so that forever after she would feel a personal connection to David and be able to take strength from him.

After they closed the Bible, Mother said, "Now, let me try. I will tell the story to you and you see if I leave out any important parts."

"Okay," said Elizabeth, straightening up and leaning forward to listen.

Mom began, "Israel was at war with the Philistines. . . ."

After she finished, having been coached in several places by Elizabeth, she said, "Okay, it's your turn."

Elizabeth began. She left several things out, but Mom made no comment, just gave Elizabeth all of her attention.

Then Mom said, "My turn," and began again, being careful to put back in the parts Elizabeth had left out. They went back and forth like this until Elizabeth's attention began to drift. Then they stopped. Another day would be just fine. The next time they sat down together, they began to create the talk using the stairs model. Then they were ready for the practicing again.

Over the next several days, at odd moments—in the car,

during Elizabeth's after-school snack, and so on—they told and retold the story to each other, probably ten or fifteen times, until the order, events, and language were all Elizabeth's own. During family home evening, Mother spontaneously asked Elizabeth to tell the story to the rest of the family while she got the refreshments ready. Another time Mother asked Elizabeth to tell the story to her younger sister, to entertain her while mother got the baby ready for bed. Mom looked for ways—spaced apart—all week for Elizabeth to tell and retell the heart of her talk. By Sunday, it was not memorized word for word, but Elizabeth was ready to really communicate, to *tell* the story to her Primary friends.

Abby was six. To get her started (exploring time), her mother asked her about her day at school. What had she done at recess? Abby was new in the school, and she began talking about asking a girl who looked nice if she could play with her. The girl said yes, and Abby was happy to have a new friend. As they talked, mother helped Abby identify her One Idea: Love one another. She wanted to tell about her new friend. As they began to create the talk, Abby wrote on her paper: "Love one another." But her mother could see that writing was laborious and she said, "Why don't you draw pictures, instead of writing words, to help you remember what you want to tell the children about loving one another?" And so Abby did.

As Abby took the next step and began to practice her talk, it was easy for her to look down, see the picture, and tell her mother, family, and eventually the Primary audience the story of being accepted by a new friend in the new school.

Abby's talk went something like this:

> I went out for recess. A girl asked me if I wanted to play. I said yes. We played on the slide. It made me feel happy to have a new friend. When someone new comes to our school, I can ask them if they want to play because Jesus said, "Love one another."

Voice

Help your child talk clearly and slowly, reminding him that what he has to tell the other children is important. Help your child understand that if he speaks too softly or too quickly, the other children will miss hearing his talk and the

Abby drew pictures of her school and of playing with a friend at recess to help her learn her talk and remember what to say next.

important things he has to say. Children love to hear their own voices in a tape recorder, and that can be a fun way to practice if you have the time and the equipment. As your child listens, then rerecords, he will naturally self-correct.

Voice has everything to do with air; and when we are nervous, we tend to breathe rapidly and shallowly and the voice doesn't work as well as it could. Explain this to your child and have him practice taking one slow, deep breath just before he practices his talk. Tell him that this is important to do when he first stands at the pulpit.

The last word of the talk, *amen*, needs to be heard. It literally means "true," and so by saying it loud and clear we indicate that we believe the things that have been said are true. Remind your child that this word is important and that he should finish saying it completely before turning around to leave the pulpit.

Posture

It is natural to speak more clearly when we stand tall. Fidgeting hands are a distraction. Sometimes just helping the child think of a good place to put his hands will be helpful.

When your child practices his talk, you may want to draw two footprints on the floor with chalk or mark two xs with tape and see if he can keep his feet in the same place for the whole talk.

Eyes

Real communicating, or "telling the talk," can't be done effectively if the child's eyes are looking down. Eye contact with people in the audience is best, but that is often difficult for beginning speakers. You might want the child to practice by looking at a picture on the wall behind the audience, or the corner of someone's chair back. That way, he looks like he is looking at the audience without becoming too self-conscious.

All of these things—voice, posture, eyes—are not as important as the other topics we have discussed. The substance and process of preparing the talk are much more valuable than the actual presentation, especially as we talk about developing portable skills. Preparation time is more likely to produce conversion and build positive relationships than the presentation itself, so don't become overly concerned about presentation skills with young children.

One Saturday morning, Nathan and James' dad took them to play basketball at the church. Dad knew that the children's sacrament meeting program was coming up and that the boys had short talks to give at the pulpit during the program. After they played ball he said, "Hey, let's go into the chapel and practice standing at the pulpit so that you will know what it feels like when you give your talks next week." Such an invitation! The boys started off full speed.

"Whoa," Dad said. "This is pretty fun, boys, but remember this is the chapel!"

As they took turns standing at the pulpit, Dad talked about what they were going to tell all of the adults in the audience, and how important the boys' messages were. "Let's figure out things we can practice this morning that will make it so they can hear and understand what you will tell them. Go sit on the benches, boys, and let me start."

Then Dad playfully demonstrated—exaggerating as much as possible—mumbling, talking very fast, and fidgeting with his clothes.

"Well, what did I say?"

They doubled over with laughter. "We couldn't hear what you said!"

"Okay, let's go to work on this one. Let's figure out some things we can do better." Then he brought them up and they each practiced standing tall, looking right at a spot on a bench in the audience, taking a deep breath before they said anything, finding a place to put their hands, and completely finishing the very last word before they turned away to sit down. When they returned home and Mom asked whether they had fun, they didn't even mention the basketball game; they couldn't wait to tell her about practicing in the chapel!

✱ ✱ ✱

Religious Identity Practicing:

• should not mean memorizing from a written text
• should be "spaced learning"—not done all at once, but over a period of days.
• should emphasize communication, or "telling the talk" to someone else
• should include some kind of prompts, such as one-word reminders on cards, one-sentence starters for each section, pictures, or other visual road maps (such as the webbed circles or four-squares discussed in the previous chapter)
• should include practice with breathing, speaking clearly and slowly, standing tall, and finding a place to look

✱ Step Four

PRESENTING THE TALK

Practice, Not Performance

In this Church, participation is not about perfected performance. We are a participatory church because we see participation as a wonderful way to learn. We don't call people to responsibilities they already know how to do; we don't expect completion of a public speaking course before someone is asked to speak or proof of a teaching certificate to become a Sunday School teacher. We believe, doctrinally, that this life is a time for practicing, for learning line upon line. That means even a finished talk shouldn't be looked at like a performance at Carnegie Hall. Presenting a talk should be viewed as a way to practice in an

> **❝** *Presenting a talk should be viewed as a way to practice in an environment of loving brothers and sisters, where we can take risks that will help us build new skills and feel together the enlightening and teaching power of the Holy Ghost.* **❞**

environment of loving brothers and sisters, where we can take risks that will help us build new skills and feel together the enlightening and teaching power of the Holy Ghost.

This is very important to communicate to your child, at every step of the process. As the actual presentation grows nearer, ask your child what would help her the most—would she like you to sit at the back? Would she like you to sit up close to her? Let her know that one of the best ways you can be helpful is by praying for her.

Make sure that prayer is a central part of that day, as it has been from the very beginning. Take time to have a private prayer before going to church. Ask the Lord to bless

* * *

Family Home Evening Fun

Impromptu preparation and speaking can be fun and instructive in family home evening lessons. This is a safe environment where family members can build confidence and skills. Besides, this kind of family home evening lesson takes almost no preparation time! Use it when the person assigned to the lesson has had a busy day. A parent or older child could team up to work with small children.

1. Choose a picture from the Church magazines or the *Gospel Art Kit.* Study the picture carefully. Think of a gospel message related to the picture. Apply it to your life. Present the talk.

2. Choose a word from the Topical Guide or Bible Dictionary. Look up one of the scriptures referred to in the entry. Explain what you think it means. Apply it to your life. Present the talk.

3. Think of something that happened to you today. Turn it into a gospel message. Apply it to your life. Present a talk.

your little speaker, as well as those in the audience. Express gratitude for the wonderful process of preparation and learning, for the gospel principle about which she will be speaking, and for the love that you have felt for each other during the preparation time.

Abby's mother said, "Remember, Abby, that you are going to be telling the other children something very important: Jesus wants us to be friendly to each other, especially to someone

"Whispering words to repeat creates dependence—your child will stop thinking and just keep waiting for you to give her the next words to repeat. It will become your talk, not hers."

who may be new at school or at church. If you get mixed up, it's okay to just start again. If you need to stop and think for a minute, that's okay too. This is such an important idea that we want to make sure you have a chance to say it, and that everyone can hear it. If you need me to help you anytime, I'll be right there. Let's pray to Heavenly Father to ask him to help you today."

When Elizabeth began to give her talk about David and Goliath, all at once her mind went blank. She looked in panic at her mother on the front row. Mother smiled, conveying calmness, not mirroring her panic, then she said quietly, "Why don't you start with the part where David goes to take his brothers some food?"

Her calmness steadied Elizabeth and directed her to start thinking again. This is so much better than whispering the next sentence. Whispering words to repeat creates dependence—your child will stop thinking and just keep waiting for you to give her the next words to repeat. It will become your talk, not hers.

It's much better to say just a few reassuring words, allowing her to stop, breathe, and refocus on the ideas she knows so well.

Once again, this is a respectful and confidence-building approach. Remember some of the skills and attributes that you want your child to develop along the way. Surely, one of those could be a growing confidence that even when your child panics, she knows she has the ability to bring it back together and continue.

✳ Magnificent Possibilities

Isn't it something? The members of Zion's Camp thought they were going to liberate the Saints in Missouri with guns and military tactics, and what the Lord had in mind was so different. He chose to use the journey as an opportunity to develop and practice fundamental, even eternal, principles. Principles as big as faith, brotherly love, charity, obedience, agency, and communication.

Those who chose to use the journey to practice these principles experienced personal growth. Joseph Smith watched the members of his camp, and from these men he chose nine of this dispensation's first twelve apostles and all of the first Quorum of the Seventy (seven presidents and sixty-three members).

Don't let your child's invitation to give a Primary talk become just another task, something to stress about, and then to have done. Think again and again of what you really want to have happen. What are some of the portable qualities your child (and you) could seek to develop along the way?

What Do You Want to Have Happen?

• Both parent and child experience the Spirit together as they discuss and pray about gospel principles and their applications. Their relationships with one another and with the Lord deepen.

• The child learns and internalizes gospel principles, understanding how the gospel applies to real life, how scriptures and the words of prophets guide his own behavior. This internalization deepens his personal identity with the gospel, helping him become more and more of who he really is at the core.

• The child learns to think for himself, gathering ideas and organizing them in meaningful ways.

• The child develops confidence in preparing and giving talks—confidence and dependability that will transfer to other situations.

• The child learns to use resources to learn, support, and illustrate gospel truths.

• The child becomes an effective teacher of the gospel, gaining the skills that will set him on the path to lifelong church service.

• As your child speaks words of truth from his heart and life, he maximizes the possibility that the Spirit will bear witness both to him and to the children in the audience.

• Testimonies are borne and strengthened, both in the speaker and the other children.

• And besides all of that, this is fun!

Enjoy.

✳ Thought Starters

Here are some topics, issues, and scripture verses that may help you and your child think up a terrific talk.

Gospel Principles and Values

- prayer
- tithing
- temples
- families
- kindness
- sacrament
- Sabbath Day
- Jesus
- the beauties of the earth

Personal Issues

- fears
- anger
- selfishness
- honesty

Scripture Verses

• "I will go and do the things which the Lord hath commanded, for I know that the Lord giveth no commandments unto the children of men, save he shall prepare a way for them that they may accomplish the thing which he commandeth them" (1 Nephi 3:7).

• "Ammon . . . began to pour out his soul in prayer and thanksgiving to God for what he had done for his brethren; and he was also overpowered with joy" (Alma 19:14).

• "Wickedness never was happiness" (Alma 41:10).

• "Fear not to do good, . . . for whatsoever ye sow, that shall ye also reap" (D&C 6:33).

• "Look unto me in every thought; doubt not, fear not" (D&C 6:36).

• "Draw near unto me and I will draw near unto you" (D&C 88:63).

• "Whatsoever we ask, we receive of him, because we keep his commandments" (1 John 3:22).